SPACE STATIONS

by Ruth Owen

PowerKiDS
press.

New York

Published in 2015 by **The Rosen Publishing Group, Inc.**
29 East 21st Street, New York, NY 10010

Library of Congress Cataloging-in-Publication Data
Owen, Ruth.
Space stations / by Ruth Owen.
p. cm. — (Objects in space)
Includes index.
ISBN 978-1-4777-5870-0 (pbk.)
ISBN 978-1-4777-5872-4 (6-pack)
ISBN 978-1-4777-5869-4 (library binding)
1. Space stations — Juvenile literature. I. Owen, Ruth, 1967-. II. Title.
TL797.15 O94 2015
629.44—d23

Produced for Rosen by Ruby Tuesday Books Ltd
Editor for Ruby Tuesday Books Ltd: Mark J. Sachner
US Editor: Sara Antill
Designer: Emma Randall
Consultant: Kevin Yates, Fellow of the Royal Astronomical Society

Photo Credits:
Cover, 1, 5, 11, 13, 15, 17, 19, 20–21, 23, 25, 27, 29 © NASA; 7 © Science Photo
Library; 9 © Public Domain.
Manufactured in the United States of America
CPSIA Compliance Information: Batch # CW15PK: For Further Information
contact Rosen Publishing, New York, New York at 1-800-237-9932

CONTENTS

A HOME IN SPACE

In science fiction movies and TV shows, vast, city-sized spacecraft or space stations move through the blackness of space. Smaller spaceships or shuttles fly to and from the mother ship like cars on a busy freeway. Thousands of people wearing identical jumpsuits go about their daily lives . . .

Today, we're still a very long way from those fictional ideas of living in space. In the 50 years since a human first flew in space, however, several space stations have successfully become homes to small crews of astronauts.

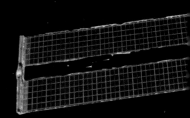

The technological challenges of building a space station, supplying it with oxygen, water, and all the other essentials for human survival, and safely transporting people back and forth from Earth have all been met. The astronauts aboard the International Space Station (ISS) even work and live alongside robots!

Space stations have helped scientists carry out exciting experiments and learn how the human body reacts to living in space. In the future, space stations **orbiting** Earth might even become stopping off points for astronauts flying to Mars.

Space stations are structures where a crew of astronauts can live. They move around Earth in a **Low Earth Orbit (LEO).** A space station does not have a means of propelling itself through space, as a spacecraft does, and it cannot land back on Earth.

The International Space Station (ISS) is the size of a football field and has as much living space as a house with six bedrooms.

SALYUT 1

The first-ever space station was built by scientists and engineers from the Soviet Union. Named Salyut 1, it was launched on April 19, 1971.

Later space stations, such as the International Space Station (JSS), were launched as individual modules that then connected together in space. The entire Salyut 1 space station was launched in one piece, however, with all its equipment aboard but no crew.

On April 22, 1971, a crew of Russian **cosmonauts** headed for the space station in a spacecraft named *Soyuz 10*. Unfortunately, the spacecraft could not dock with Salyut 1, and the mission was aborted. On June 6, 1971, a second crew launched on *Soyuz 11*. They successfully docked with Salyut 1 and became the first humans to board a space station.

After 23 days living on Salyut 1, the crew had to cut their mission short. The space station was experiencing problems, so the cosmonauts climbed into *Soyuz 11* and headed back to Earth.

SPACE OBJECTS FACT FILE

Salyut 1 was 52 feet (15.8 m) long. It orbited Earth at just a little over 100 miles (160 km) above the planet's surface.

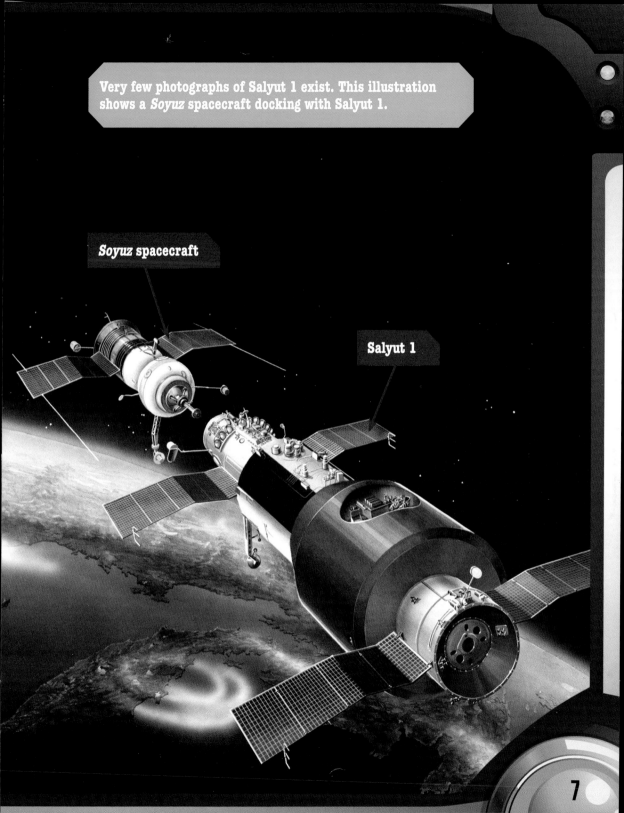

Very few photographs of Salyut 1 exist. This illustration shows a *Soyuz* spacecraft docking with Salyut 1.

Soyuz spacecraft

Salyut 1

SALYUT–SUCCESS AND TRAGEDY

Following their pioneering 23-day stay aboard Salyut 1, the *Soyuz 11* crew headed for home.

The spacecraft re-entered Earth's **atmosphere** and landed using parachutes. Tragically, when the recovery team reached Soyuz 11, they found all three crew members dead. A malfunction inside the spacecraft had caused the crew to suffocate. At the time, cosmonauts did not wear protective pressure suits, or spacesuits, that supplied them with oxygen during flights.

All missions to *Salyut 1* were suspended while scientists redesigned the *Soyuz* spacecraft to allow cosmonauts to fly wearing pressure suits. No cosmonaut ever visited Salyut 1 again. After 175 days in orbit, ground control put the space station into a lower orbit so it fell back to Earth and burned up in Earth's atmosphere.

Over time, the Soviet Union's Salyut program successfully launched six space stations that spent time in orbit with cosmonauts aboard. Salyut 1, 4, 6, and 7 were used for scientific research missions. Salyut 3 and 5 carried out secret military missions.

SPACE OBJECTS FACT FILE

The three brave cosmonauts who were the first humans to live on a space station were Georgi Dobrovolski, Viktor Patsayev, and Vladislav Volkov.

A stamp from the Soviet Union commemorating the *Soyuz 11* cosmonauts. The caption says, "A feat by heroes will live on for centuries."

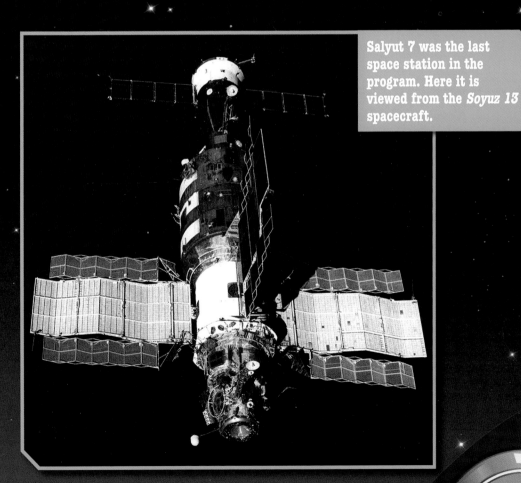

Salyut 7 was the last space station in the program. Here it is viewed from the *Soyuz 13* spacecraft.

THE STORY OF SKYLAB

On May 14, 1973, the space agency NASA launched the first U.S. space station, Skylab.

As Skylab launched, however, it suffered some damage. One of its arrays of **solar panels** was torn off and the second array jammed so it could not be deployed. The incident also damaged some of the space station's protection against the Sun's heat. Skylab went into orbit unable to produce electricity and in serious danger of overheating.

On May 25, 1973, Skylab-2 (SL-2), the first manned mission to Skylab, was launched. The three-man crew traveled to Skylab in a Command/Service Module (CSM) spacecraft—the same type of spacecraft that carried astronauts to the Moon. The SL-2 crew had been trained to fix the space station. The astronauts deployed an umbrella-like sunshade and made a spacewalk to fix the jammed solar array. Once Skylab was repaired, the crew moved into their new home!

After the first Skylab mission, two more successful manned missions were made. SL-3 launched on July 28, 1973, and SL-4 launched later that same year on November 16.

SPACE OBJECTS FACT FILE

At just over 86 feet (26 m) long, Skylab was nearly the length of a basketball court and just slightly wider. With a weight of 169,950 pounds (77,088 kg), the space station weighed as much as 34 SUVs.

Skylab-3 astronaut Owen K. Garriott deploys scientific equipment to the outside of the space station during the SL-3 mission.

This photo of Skylab was taken by the SL-4 crew as they departed.

DAILY LIFE ON SKYLAB

The Skylab space station included a workshop, a solar observatory, or telescope, and living quarters. Three people could live on board for 84 days.

The astronauts' days included meals, work, free time, and 90 minutes of exercise. Astronauts worked out by riding a stationary bike or jogging around the station's water tank. A favorite free-time activity was looking at Earth from Skylab's window.

A large part of each day was spent working. The three Skylab crews studied the Sun using the space station's solar observatory. They also carried out 2,000 hours of experiments. The plan for each day's experiments was sent from ground control. When the astronauts printed it out on their teleprinter, the list of instructions was sometimes nearly 50 feet (15 m) long.

Many of the experiments studied how the astronauts' bodies reacted to living in space. The crew tested their urine, stool, blood, bones, cells, and sleep patterns. They also tested how mice and gnats responded to being in space, where there is no day or night.

SPACE OBJECTS FACT FILE

Skylab spent 2,249 days in orbit. When its mission was over, it re-entered Earth's atmosphere on July 11, 1979. Most of the station burned up, but some pieces fell to Earth, landing in Western Australia.

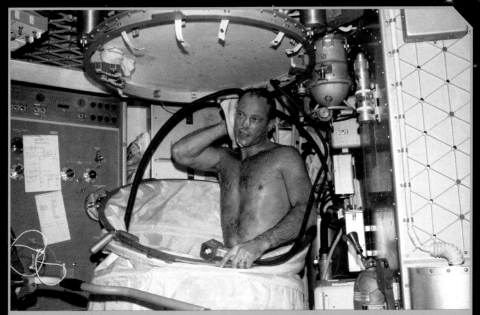

SL-3 astronaut Jack R. Lousma takes a shower on Skylab.

SL-3 astronaut Owen K. Garriott strapped into his sleep restraints at bedtime.

THE MIR SPACE STATION

The Soviet Union's Salyut program paved the way for Mir, an ambitious and highly challenging space station project. Built by the Soviet Union, Mir became the property of Russia after the Soviet Union broke up into independent nations in 1991.

Unlike Salyut, Mir was constructed from seven modules that were launched one by one and then fitted together in space. The first core module, Mir DOS-7, was launched aboard a rocket on February 20, 1986. The other modules followed throughout the late 1980s and 1990s, until the final section was added in 1996. Like Mir DOS-7, each module was launched on a rocket. Once in orbit, it "chased" the space station until it was in position to connect to the main core module.

Mir spent 5,519 days, over 15 years, in orbit around Earth with a crew on board for 4,592 of those days. The first crew arrived on July 16, 1986. In the years that followed, 28 long-duration crews would live on the space station, with an average mission lasting about six months.

SPACE OBJECTS FACT FILE

A Mir crew member had a small booth called a Kayutka. Each booth had a sleeping bag securely fixed to one side, a foldout desk, a porthole window, and storage for the crew member's personal items.

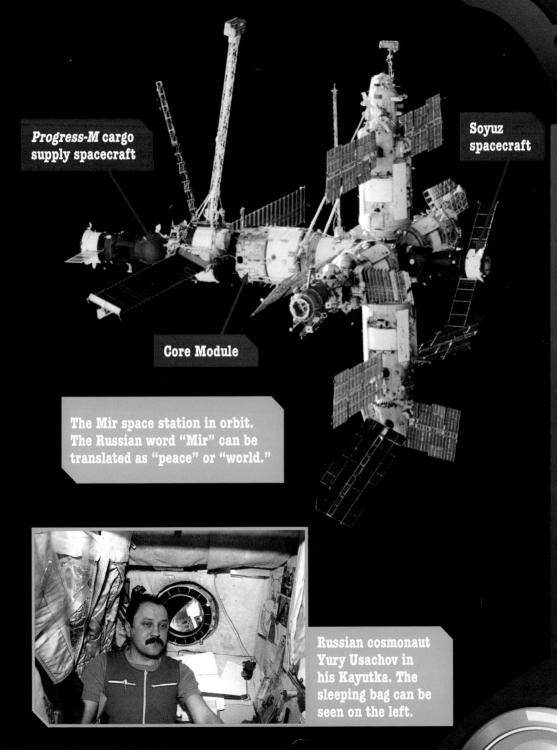

Progress-M cargo
supply spacecraft

Soyuz
spacecraft

Core Module

The Mir space station in orbit.
The Russian word "Mir" can be
translated as "peace" or "world."

Russian cosmonaut
Yury Usachov in
his Kayutka. The
sleeping bag can be
seen on the left.

15

SUCCESSES AND FAILURES

During the Mir space station's time in orbit, 104 people from 12 different nations visited the space station. Astronauts from Europe, Japan, and the United States all worked alongside the Russian cosmonauts.

Life on board Mir didn't always run smoothly, and several accidents happened. In February 1997, a malfunction caused a fire that burned for around 90 seconds, filling the station with toxic smoke.

In June 1997, the *Progress M-34*, an unmanned cargo spacecraft, was carrying out docking tests. It crashed into the space station's module named *Spektr*, seriously damaging that section. The module had to be shut down and permanently sealed off.

In March 2001, after 15 years in orbit, Mir's time in space came to an end. A spacecraft named *Progress M1-5* docked to Mir and by firing its engines, slowed down the space station. This made Mir drop into a lower orbit so it fell back into Earth's atmosphere. Most of the space station disintegrated on re-entry, with some fragments falling into the Pacific Ocean.

SPACE OBJECTS FACT FILE

The Mir space station holds the record for the longest single human spaceflight. Cosmonaut Valeri Polyakov spent 437 days and 18 hours on Mir.

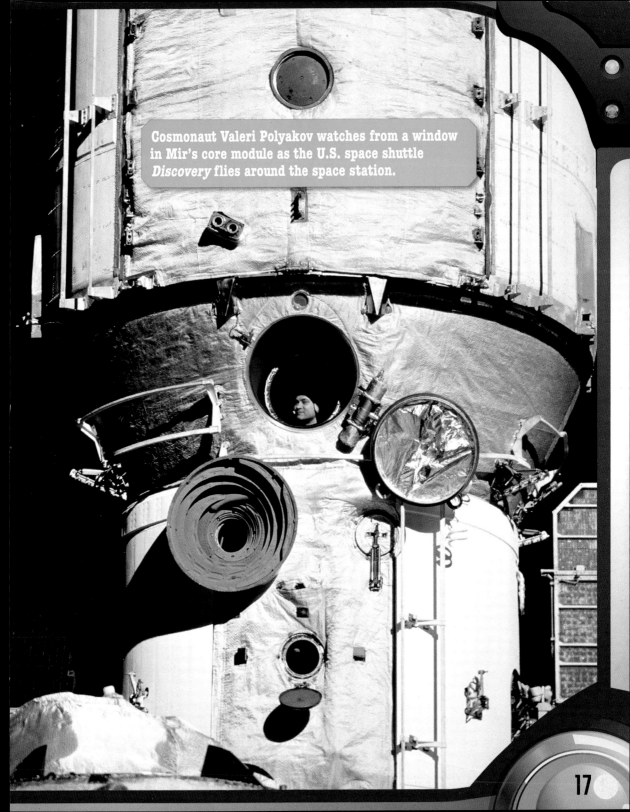

Cosmonaut Valeri Polyakov watches from a window in Mir's core module as the U.S. space shuttle *Discovery* flies around the space station.

THE INTERNATIONAL SPACE STATION (ISS)

On November 20, 1998, a Russian-built space station module named *Zarya* was launched and went into orbit. The construction in space of the International Space Station (ISS) had begun!

Like Mir, the ISS is a modular space station. It is bigger than Mir, however, and is the largest artificial structure in space. It can even be seen from Earth with the naked eye!

Some ISS modules were blasted into space by Russian *Proton* and *Soyuz* rockets. These modules then flew into position. Other modules were carried to the ISS by U.S. space shuttles. Following the successful launch of *Zarya*, in December 1998, the space shuttle *Endeavour* carried the second module, *Unity*, into space and made the first connection between two ISS units. As construction of the space station continued over the next decade, many more modules and pieces of equipment were carried into space on more than 115 flights.

Once completed, the space station weighed more than 180 SUVs. Its wing-like solar arrays were longer than the wingspan of a Boeing 777 airliner.

SPACE OBJECTS FACT FILE

The ISS is a joint project between five space agencies: NASA, Roscosmos (Russian Federal Space Agency), ESA (European Space Agency), JAXA (Japan Aerospace Exploration Agency), and the CSA (Canadian Space Agency).

The first two modules of the International Space Station (ISS), *Zarya* (top) and *Unity* (bottom).

The interior of the *Zarya* module.

GETTING TO THE ISS

The first crew arrived at the International Space Station (ISS) on November 2, 2000.

Named Expedition 1, the mission's crew was made up of two Russian cosmonauts and one U.S. astronaut. Since that day, people have lived on the ISS continuously.

During its lifetime, ISS crews have traveled to and from the space station in U.S. space shuttles and Russian *Soyuz* spacecraft. Cargo, such as equipment for experiments, food, and even the space station's robot crew members, have been delivered by space shuttles and *Soyuz* craft, and also by Japanese and European unmanned spacecraft.

Since the U.S. space shuttle program ended, *Soyuz* spacecraft alone carry crews to and from the ISS. A *Soyuz* spacecraft takes six hours to reach the space station. Its return journey takes just three and a half hours.

Most missions to the ISS have been launched by government-run space agencies. In 2012, a *Dragon* spacecraft became the first **commercial** spacecraft to carry cargo to the ISS. The spacecraft was developed by a U.S. company, SpaceX.

This photo, taken by a crew member on a *Soyuz* spacecraft, shows the space shuttle *Endeavour* docked with the ISS.

SPACE OBJECTS FACT FILE

If there's an emergency on the space station, the crew can use a *Soyuz* spacecraft to escape back to Earth. Like a ship's lifeboat, one *Soyuz* remains docked with the ISS at all times.

Space shuttle
Endeavour

SPACE STATION ESSENTIALS

Hundreds of different challenges have to be solved by technology in order for humans to live in space. Making oxygen and water are just two of these. Keeping a space station crew healthy is also extremely important.

Onboard the International Space Station (ISS), most of the oxygen is supplied by the Elektron system which turns water into breathable oxygen. Water is made up of molecules of hydrogen and oxygen. Elektron takes water, for example waste water from washing, and separates the molecules into the two gases. The oxygen is pumped into the station for breathing and the hydrogen is vented into space. The Elektron system was also used on Mir.

One way to obtain enough drinking water is to recycle wastewater. On the ISS, even the crew's urine is cleaned and recycled back into fresh water.

On a space station, crew members experience zero **gravity** (or weightlessness). Floating around looks like fun, but low gravity makes an astronaut's muscles and bones grow weak. Scientists study the ISS crew members to learn how their bodies are affected by living in a weightless environment.

SPACE OBJECTS FACT FILE

People living in zero gravity must exercise to keep their bones and muscles strong. Crew members onboard the ISS exercise for two hours every day.

ISS crew members work out on treadmills, a stationary bike, and resistance equipment. Here, astronaut Sunita Williams is strapped to a treadmill with bungee cords as she runs.

These ISS crew members are drinking water that was once urine!

EVERYDAY LIFE ON THE ISS

The crew members on the International Space Station (ISS) spend their days working. They also exercise, relax, sleep, and do everyday things like eating and going to the bathroom.

The crew's food must last for long periods of time. Cans are too heavy to transport to space, so the food is vacuum sealed for long life in plastic bags. Each crew member warms up his or her own food in the station's small galley, or kitchen. Drinks and soups are supplied as powders in small plastic bags. Water is added to the powder and then the liquid is sipped through a straw to keep globs of drink or soup from floating into the air and contaminating equipment.

Washing and going to the bathroom are both tricky when you are weightless. When washing, crew members use a handheld water jet to spray water onto their bodies. They also use wet wipes. The ISS toilets have seatbelt-like straps so the crew members can strap themselves to the toilet. You wouldn't want to float off halfway through!

SPACE OBJECTS FACT FILE

The toothpaste used on the ISS is edible so that crew members do not need to rinse their mouths and use up precious water.

When a supplies spacecraft arrives from Earth, the ISS crew gets to enjoy fruit, vegetables, and other fresh foods for a short while. Here, astronauts are making hamburgers.

Different types of foods are supplied for crew members from different nations. This package contains vacuum-packed ramen noodles and soy sauce prepared for Japanese astronauts.

THE ROBOT CREW

The crew of the International Space Station (ISS) gets plenty of help with its tasks from the station's robot crew.

Canadarm2 is a large robotic arm that operates on the outside of the ISS. It is 57.7 feet (17.6 m) long and has seven joints, or bends. When new sections of the ISS are delivered by spacecraft, Canadarm2 can maneuver them into position. During spacewalks to make repairs to the space station's exterior, Canadarm2 can move astronauts into place, too.

Robonaut is a humanoid robot that is being tested on the ISS. Because it is the shape and size of a human, it may one day work alongside people and fit into places designed for human crew members.

Using robots to repair the exterior of the ISS reduces the amount of dangerous spacewalks that astronauts must make. Robots, such as Robonaut, might one day take over everyday tasks such as replacing batteries and running daily equipment checks. This will leave astronauts free for carrying out important scientific work.

SPACE OBJECTS FACT FILE

Dextre is a second robot designed to work on the outside of the ISS. Dextre has two arms that are each 11 feet (3.4 m) long. Tools can be fitted to the ends of the arms like fingers.

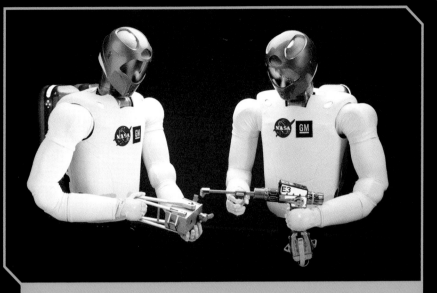

A Robonaut's hands can use tools designed for people and carry out delicate tasks.

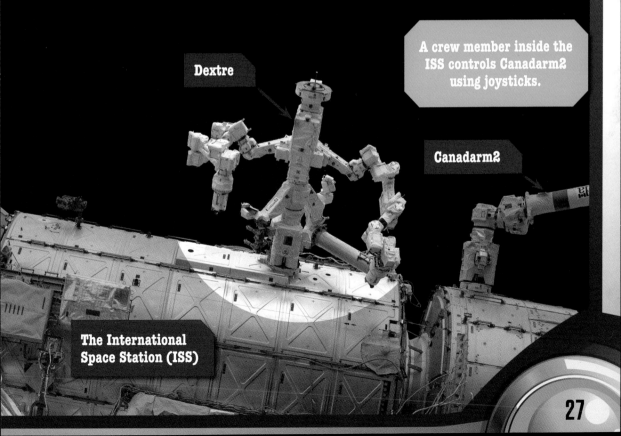

A crew member inside the ISS controls Canadarm2 using joysticks.

Dextre

Canadarm2

The International Space Station (ISS)

SCIENCE IN SPACE

For more than 14 years, the International Space Station (ISS) has been used as a laboratory in space.

Crew members have carried out many hundreds of experiments in fields such as **astronomy, meteorology,** and human biology. Being able to work in an environment where there is no gravity has led scientists to make important discoveries. For example, scientists found that bacteria act differently outside of Earth's gravity. This has led to new developments in ways to treat diseases. The ISS and other space stations have also allowed scientists to study the long-term effects of space travel on the human body.

Building space stations where humans can safely live has been an incredible technological achievement. We have learned a huge amount from the brave men and women that have lived on these structures. In the future, space stations orbiting Earth might become stopping off points for spacecraft on their way to Mars. They may even become orbital construction yards where spacecraft are built for missions that will travel much farther into our **solar system**.

SPACE OBJECTS FACT FILE

The ISS has been used as a place where **engineers** can test out new spacecraft and other pieces of equipment that might one day be used for missions to the Moon or Mars.

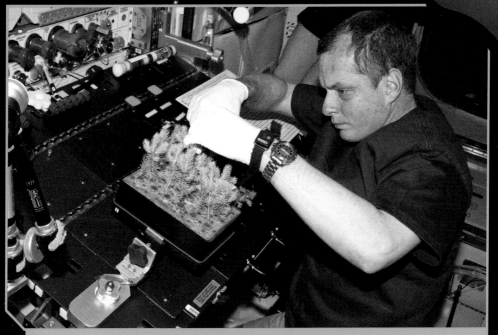

ISS astronaut T.J. Creamer experiments with growing trees in space.

A group of astronauts from around the world enjoys a meal together on the ISS.

GLOSSARY

astronomy
(uh-STRAH-nuh-mee) The scientific study of space.

atmosphere
(AT-muh-sfeer) The layer of gases surrounding a planet, moon, or star.

commercial
(cuh-MUR-shul) Done by a business in order to make money.

cosmonauts
(KAHZ-muh-nawtz) Astronauts from Russia, and before 1991 from the Soviet Union.

engineers
(en-jun-NIHRZ) People who use math, science, and technology to design and build machines such as cars and spacecraft. Some engineers design and build structures such as skyscrapers and bridges.

gravity
(GRA-vuh-tee) The force that causes objects to be attracted toward Earth's center or toward other physical bodies in space, such as stars or planets.

laboratory
(LA-bruh-tor-ee) A room, building, or sometimes a vehicle where there is equipment that can be used to carry out experiments and other scientific studies.

Low Earth Orbit (LEO)
(LOH ERTH OR-bit) Orbiting Earth at a height between 100 and 1,250 miles (160–2,000 km) above Earth's surface.

meteorology
(mee-tee-uh-RAH-luh-jee) The scientific study of Earth's atmosphere and the events, such as weather, that take place there.

orbiting
(OR-bih-ting) Moving, or traveling, around another object in a curved path.

solar panels
(SOH-ler PA-nulz) Panels made up of a number of solar cells that capture the Sun's energy and use it to make power, such as electricity.

solar system
(SOH-ler SIS-tem) The Sun and everything that orbits around it, including planets and their moons, asteroids, meteoroids, and comets.

Soviet Union
(SOH-vee-et YOON-yun) A former nation made up of a group of republics in parts of Europe and Asia. The Soviet Union broke up in 1991, creating a group of independent nations, including Russia, Ukraine, Kazakhstan, and Georgia.

WEBSITES

Due to the changing nature of Internet links, PowerKids Press has developed an online list of websites related to the subject of this book. This site is updated regularly. Please use this link to access the list: www.powerkidslinks.com/ois/stat

READ MORE

Hamilton, Laura Waxman. *Exploring the International Space Station*. Minneapolis, MN: Lerner Publishing Group, 2012.

Throp, Claire. *Visit to a Space Station*. Chicago: Raintree, 2014.

Zappa, Maria. *Space Stations*. Edina, MN: ABDO Publishing, 2011.

INDEX